For Isabella and Toby

Copyright © 2025 by Stephanie Lipsey-Liu.
All rights reserved
No part of this publication may be reproduced or transmitted in any form or by any means, electronic or mechanical, including photocopying, recording, scanning or otherwise, or through any information browsing, storage or retrieval system, without permission in writing from the publisher.

 First printed 2025

ISBN 978-1-7399336-8-5
Little Lion Publishing UK
Nottingham, England
www.littlelionpublishing.co.uk

The following collective nouns you are about to learn are the real names for each group!

Happy learning!

This Little Lion book belongs to

....

A mischief of elves

Elves work hard, but when they're done:

it's time to party, so let's have fun!

LIST OF ELF DUTIES

LOOK AFTER SANTA'S REINDEER

MAKE SURE THE SLEIGH WORKS PROPERLY

HELP SANTA WITH HIS "NAUGHTY OR NICE" LIST

MAKE TOYS

How many elves do you think it takes to help Father Christmas make all the toys?

A round of robins

The robins sing and tweet their song,

they love to make noise all day long!

Have you ever heard someone say "robin red-breast"?

A robin actually has a patch of orange feathers, not red. When this name was first used many years ago, the colour orange didn't have a name yet! So red was the closest word they could use to describe it.

Did you know?

Robins lay blue eggs!

A round of robins can have as many as 200,000 birds in it! However, this only usually happens in winter when there is a shortage of food.

A bevy of partridges

In a pear tree? I don't think so!

They nest on the ground, way down low.

Partridges don't often fly and they build their nests on the ground. So in the song "The Twelve Days of Christmas," the partridge probably wasn't really in a pear tree!

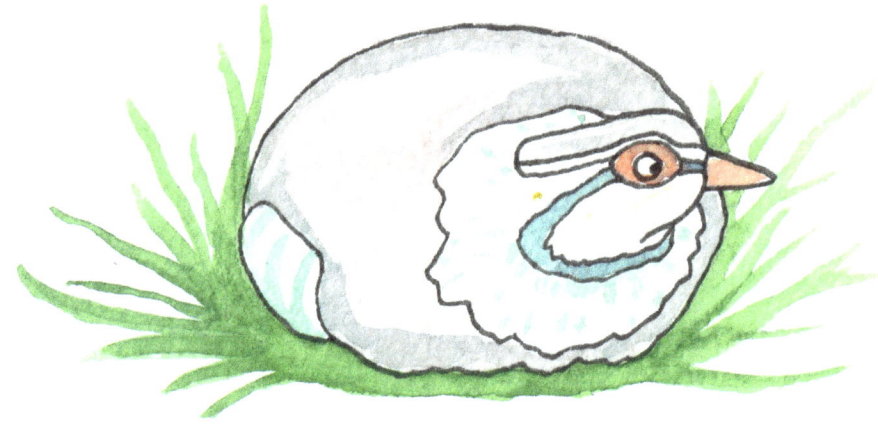

Did you know? Quails and larks are also known as a bevy!

Can you remember what a group of elves is called?
Turn back to page 1 to see if you got it right!

A blizzard of snowy owls

Owls hunt at night and sleep in the day,

but for the snowys it's the other way!

Most owls are nocturnal, but snowy owls are different; they are diurnal, like humans! This means they are awake during the day and sleep at night.

Snowy owls eat lots of lemmings;
as many as 1,600 in a year!
Sometimes they save some for later,
when food is harder to find.

Can you remember what a group of robins is called?
Turn back to page 3 to see if you got it right!

A gang of turkeys

That turkey, is it a girl or a boy?

Just look at its poop: for a boy, it's a "J"!

Female turkeys poo in a spiral shape, and male turkeys poo in the shape of the letter "J"!

Male turkeys are called gobblers, and females are called hens. A group of wild turkeys is called a gang, while a group of farm turkeys is called a flock.

Can you remember what a group of partridges is called? Turn back to page 5 to see if you got it right!

A herd of reindeer

So many reindeer pull the sleigh,

with presents and toys to give away.

Reindeer were among the first animals to make friends with humans over 2,000 years ago!

Both male and female reindeer grow antlers, but males lose theirs in November. Females keep theirs all winter, which means the reindeer pulling Santa's sleigh are all girl reindeer!

Can you remember what a group of snowy owls is called? Turn back to page 7 to see if you got it right!

A truelove of turtle doves

Have you ever seen a turtle dove?

On the ground, or high above?

Unfortunately, there aren't as many turtle doves around anymore.

They eat seeds from weeds, but humans often dig up and throw them away, so there isn't much food left for the doves.

Turtle doves can fly long distances, mostly at night.
They can fly as far as 700 km without stopping.
That's from London to Edinburgh and a little further!

Can you remember what a group of turkeys is called?
Turn back to page 9 to see if you got it right!

A gaggle of geese

Christmas Day, goose for lunch?

Or duck or turkey, what will you munch?

"Goose" is actually the name for a female goose. Male geese are called ganders, and baby geese are called goslings.

Fossils show that geese have been around for 10 to 12 million years!

Can you remember what a group of reindeer is called? Turn back to page 11 to see if you got it right!

A hug of teddy bears

A hug of teddies, blue or brown,

surely the sweetest collective noun!

The term "teddy bear" came from an American president called Teddy Roosevelt. He went on a hunting trip and refused to shoot a bear.

Thankfully, he wouldn't let anyone else shoot it either.

If you thought you had a lot of toys, how about 20,367 teddy bears? That's the latest world record for the most teddy bears in one collection!

Can you remember what a group of turtle doves is called? Turn back to page 13 to see if you got it right!

A chorus of angels

A chorus of angels fill the sky,
their voices lifting soft and high.

Angels are mentioned in many religions.

They are believed to carry messages to humans from a higher power. Traditional pictures show angels with halos above their heads and wings on their backs, but some people say they can change shape and appear in human form.

Can you remember what a group of geese is called?
Turn back to page 15 to see if you got it right!

A melt of snowmen

Roll up the snow and pat, pat, pat!

Two eyes of coal and a woolly hat!

The largest snowman ever made was 122 feet tall and had trees for arms.

That's as tall as six houses stacked on top of each other!

Did you know?
Every flake of snow has 6 points?

Can you remember the name for a teddy bears?
Turn back to page 17 to see if you were right!

A drove of donkeys

Mary and Joseph on Christmas Eve night,
followed the path of a star so bright.

The story of the birth of Jesus in the Bible doesn't actually say that Mary rode a donkey to Bethlehem.

It's much more likely that she travelled by horse or camel.

Did you know?
If a donkey goes blind, it will make friends with another donkey that acts as its guide.

Can you remember what a group of angels is called?
Turn back to page 19 to see if you got it right!

An assembly of toys

The mischievous elves are making toys for all the good girls and boys!

We often think of an assembly as the meeting at the start of the school day. Assembly can also mean to make something, like a toy!

Did you know?

The oldest known doll is 4,000 years old!

The first electric toy invented was a toy train.

Can you remember what a group of snowmen is called?

Turn back to page 21 to see if you got it right!

Glossary

Blind:

Having very poor central or side vision, or sometimes no eyesight at all.

Blizzard:

A huge snowstorm with strong winds.

Chorus:

Like a choir, a group of singers.

Collective noun:

The name for a group of things, animals, or people.

Fossil:

The preserved remains of dead animals from millions of years ago, usually found in rocks.

Mischief:

Playful naughtiness, often done by children.

 Can you remember what a group of donkeys is called? Turn back to page 23 to see if you got it right!

About the Author

Stephanie was born on the Wirral and now lives in Nottingham with her husband, daughter, dogs, rabbits and hamster. She is an optician but when she is not testing eyes she can be found sewing, playing the harp, practising sign language, singing and/or adventuring with her family.

About the Illlustrator

Jemma was born in Wiltshire in England but now lives in Cardiff in Wales with her fiancée and pounce of cats. When she's not drawing or teaching her lovely little learners, she can be found campervanning, kayaking and climbing mountains.

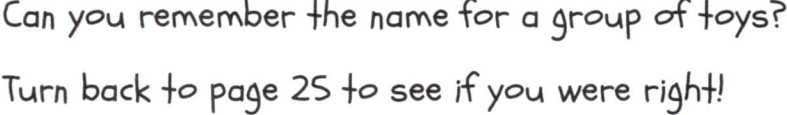

Can you remember the name for a group of toys?

Turn back to page 25 to see if you were right!

If you enjoyed a Mischief of Elves, look out for our other collective noun books.

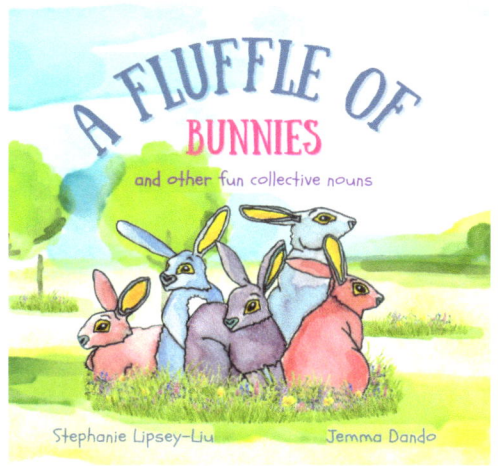
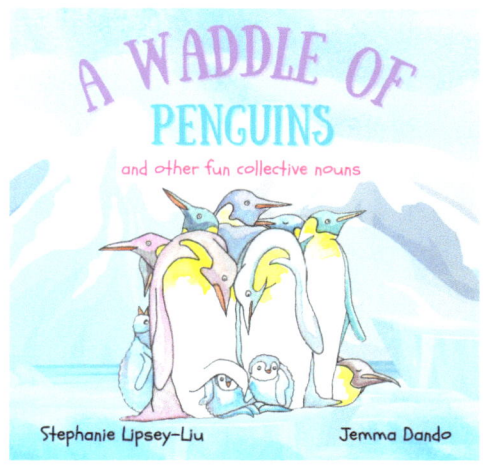
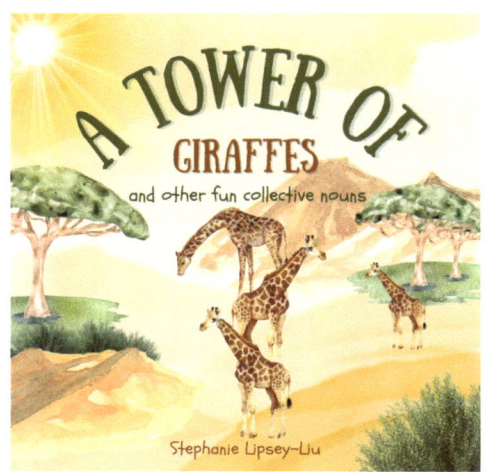

We would LOVE it if you could leave us a review on Amazon! Get your adult to help you with what to write. If you would like to share a picture of you reading a Fluffle of Bunnies, please tag us on facebook @littlelionpublishinguk or on instagram @littlelionpublishing.

www.ingramcontent.com/pod-product-compliance
Lightning Source LLC
Chambersburg PA
CBHW041106070526
44583CB00002B/83